Military Contractor's Handbook
How to get Hired
. . . and Survive

By
Derek Miller

Contents

Prologue

"Please come with us." The Afghan intelligence officer said. "We need to talk to you at the police station."

He stood a few feet inside the gate of our heavily guarded civilian compound in Kabul. It was August and the cruel Afghanistan sun blazed down upon all of us who were standing around him. We were all baking, sweat pouring out of every inch of our bodies, but I knew he had to be suffering the most. His ill-fitting black suit jacket hung off his small body which I figured he had probably chosen in order to look more official when he came to interrogate us. It had not been a wise choice in this weather.

He looked tired. I could understand why. It was around two o'clock in the afternoon and being Muslim, he had no doubt been observing Ramadan. If he was being strictly observant of this time of religious fasting, he had not taken a drink of liquid or a bite of food since sunrise. It would be many more hours before he could taste cool liquid in the miserably hot weather and he was not in a good mood. Nor were the four Afghan police officers he had brought with him.

"What is all this about?" Our deputy program manager drew himself up to his full imposing height. He used to be a cop and knew how to look intimidating as well but the intelligence officer did not appear to be impressed.

I was not amused. This was deadly serious. We never knew who might be our friend...or foe... in this crazy war. One of the Taliban's favorite tricks was to steal official uniforms and use them to sneak onto secure compounds. They could then start shooting people at random.

"It will only take three minutes of your time," the intelligence officer insisted. He kept shoving a piece of paper written in Farsi at us. "This is a letter requesting for three of your men to come to the police district headquarters to answer questions," he told the deputy program manager.

It could have been a recipe for cookies for all I knew. Or an order to have us beheaded.

I was fairly certain I knew exactly what this was

about. A disgruntled employee who had resigned the day before had shown up unannounced back at our compound. She was already known as a trouble maker with the compound leaders and our management team. She claimed we had stolen personal items from her room. We of, course, had made sure no one had been alone with her personal belongings as we packed them up to mail back to the US for her. Plus, there were many, many video cameras all over the camp recording every movement and we could prove our coming and going and what we were or were not carrying with us from place to place.

Instead of going through proper channels to let her complaint be known, she went off site to the Afghan police station and filed false criminal charges. This matter could have been easily handled internally, but she knew that the proper channels would see her charges in the context of her dismissal the day before. So she took advantage of her dual citizenship (Afghan-US) and went to the Afghanis who had no idea what she was up to.

She had either bribed someone or maybe one of her many boyfriends had connections with a local government office. Either way, she had lied and was trying to get three people in trouble. And not just in trouble as in losing jobs. She was trying to get three people killed.

Frantic calls were being made. It seemed everyone

around me was calling the US Military, US Embassy, and anyone else who could possibly help. We knew we did not fall under Afghan law and we knew "three minutes" could easily turn into three months of being in one of the worst prisons in the world.

Everyone we called was either in a meeting or was not picking up the phone.

Our only defense was to delay and hope that the officer and his back-up would give up and go home. This was an internal matter. There was no need for Afghan officials to get involved in a matter of an American civilian making false accusations against other Americans.

For reasons none of us understood, the intelligence officer did not want to give up. He needed something to take back to headquarters to show for his efforts. Two hours later we were still roasting in the sun and nothing had been accomplished except that this piece of paper had gone from being an "invitation letter" to being called a "warrant" to arrest three of our employees and I was one of those employees.

At this point, it was a stare-down. We had our private security detail standing next to us, guns at the ready, highly- trained and all had been in combat before. These were not "rent-a-cops". It was their job to protect us at all cost. They were not small guys. They worked out every day and if there was 1% of body fat on them I would be surprised. All muscle and ready to defend us. Frankly, just one of them could have snapped all five of the supposed Afghan officials in half with their bare hands. We never went anywhere without them, but we knew that if we went to the police headquarters where the intelligence officer was determined to take us, they would be blocked from coming.

Finally, a visiting corporate manager who had been in the Middle East for a long time took us aside and in a low voice mentioned the name of a US base within driving distance of us. "Get out of here. Now," he said. "You need protection that I can't give you, but US Military Police can help. I'll try to keep them busy." With him distracting the intelligence officer and the other officers we passed through the protective wall of our security detail. They drew their shoulders wide to block the view of us walking through a small door. Once out of sight, we grabbed our bug-out bags, passports, and our emergency cash. We then ran to an up-armored vehicle that our security team had standing by and drove like bats out of hell to the US Military Police for assistance. It was our only hope.

We made it to the base and obviously I am not writing from an Afghan prison. But all should note that strange, unpredictable, dangerous things can happen in any war zone. If you have any thought of working as a military contractor employee, there are some basic things you need to know. That's what this book is about.

Chapter One

Contract Work

You might have heard about the $100,000 jobs working as military contractors overseas, and they do exist. You may be drawn by the money, adventure, sense of duty to your country or other personal reasons. This book is to give you an idea of the good, the bad, and the ugly of the realities of working overseas as a contractor. It will also give you real-life advice on how to get a good paying job overseas as a contractor and what life might be like after you obtain employment.

I remember well getting on that plane stateside the first time. The itinerary was New York to Paris, and then to Dubai. I remember trying to act macho and in control, but the reality was I had butterflies in my stomach from wondering what the heck to expect next. Unlike many contractors, I had no military experience or military training. All I had was a hard-won MBA, a wife and two kids to support, and a debt load scarier than my fear of getting kidnapped by the Taliban.

So what makes me qualified to write this book? I have nineteen years of HR experience, a BA in Human Resources, an MBA in Human Resources and five years working directly as a Human Resource Generalist and HR Manager in Afghanistan for various projects. I've also logged hundreds of hours flying over the Atlantic Ocean coming home for R&R every three months to see my wife and kids. I've lived in tents, plywood boxes, and storage containers. I've survived mortar attacks, suicide bombs, bad food, loneliness, self-doubt, and cobras.

I've also paid off those debts, put money in the bank, own a nice house in the States, missed too many soccer games and birthdays to count...and worried about losing my marriage and kids in the process.

This book is to help whoever might read this to evaluate and weigh both the risks and the rewards of overseas contract work.

Chapter Two

How It Happened

I was in my mid-thirties, sitting at my desk doing a decent job as a Senior Human Resource Specialist for a large auto parts manufacturing company. However, I was quietly upset about having been recently passed up for a once-in-a-lifetime management training opportunity. They only had one opening for this special training and I had come in second, which had hurt my feelings—a situation that seems almost laughable to me now.

Don't get me wrong, I worked for a great company, but we were living in Michigan six hours away from any family. My wife was from Texas so the cold was a huge adjustment for her. Plus, we were living in a small apartment with two kids, school debt, credit card debt, car payment, hardly anything saved for retirement, etc. The normal stuff young couples deal with.

Money was tight and now that I knew for sure I had

not gotten the management training position, I did not see many options. So I was trying to cheer myself up by reading an email distribution list I had been on for years about potential HR jobs. About this time, a job popped up, "Want to work in Iraq or Afghanistan and make over $100,000?"

Well sure! $100,000 looked like a fortune to me. I did some quick calculations. With that much money coming in, we could live well and pay everything off easily in about two years! I submitted my resume, fully expecting to hear nothing back. Instead, to my shock, three days later I got a call, was interviewed for fifteen minutes, and then was asked, "When can you start?"

I was stunned. It felt like I had accidentally proposed to a woman I had just met and she had accepted before I knew whether or not I wanted to be married to her. I was so stunned I nearly walked into a wall going out to my car. Here I was, hired, and going overseas. My whole world tilted permanently after only a fifteen-minute interview.

Three weeks later, after a week-long training session in Texas, I was on a plane to Dubai.

Dubai is a sort of oasis to those of us who work in the Middle East. Dubai has been described as the Paris of the Middle East. I heard they sent architects to Las Vegas to learn how to build a city in the middle of a desert. It does have a Vegas feel but instead of walking anywhere, you want to take a taxi or ride the metro. It is hot!

I had not been told what country I would go to after Dubai. I was informed I would be told my next destination once I checked in at Dubai. It was all very secretive and wisely so. The Taliban have ears everywhere. Still, I felt like I was suddenly in the middle of a Mission Impossible movie. I would not have been particularly surprised if a self-destructing message had appeared saying, "Your mission, should you choose to accept it…"

Don't get me wrong. At the time I already considered myself a bit of a world traveler. I had lived in Japan and Canada and had traveled to other countries, but going into the Middle East during a war was overwhelming to say the least. When I reached Dubai, instead of a self-destructing message, I was told to report to a meeting room. There were probably about thirty of us in the room. One by one they called us up and told us our destination and what time to catch our flight. We only had about four hours to catch our next flight. I was told I was going to Bagram Airbase. I asked if that was my final destination and was told I would be informed of my final destination once I got to Bagram.

It was like flying into Mars on the approach to Bagram. We were warned we might have to do tactical landing. That is where your plane may go into a tight spin downward over the airport to give the bad guys less time to launch a missile at you. I looked out the window at the alien landscape. Sand and rocks everywhere you looked. Finally, "mud" houses came into view along with craters that had been formed by bombs. I don't think I blinked the whole time on approach and landing.

We landed and lined up single file off the airfield. Later, I would learn that every few flights there would always be someone who refused to get off the plane and would have to be flown back to Dubai.

Once I landed at Bagram us "newbies" were herded into a tent where our personal belongings were searched to make sure we were not bringing in contraband items. About five minutes after being in the tent I heard an explosion in the distance. I'll admit I flinched and thought "What the heck am I doing here?" None of the experienced people seem to panic so I didn't. I did ask what that was.

"Oh, that was probably a mine going off," one of the soldiers standing near me said. "You will learn the difference between those type of explosions and incoming explosions."

I never did learn the difference; I still flinch every time I hear an explosion and I get ready for anything.

After Bagram, I was flown to a place called Chagh-charan, a NATO compound situated in the poorest province in the poorest nation in the world. I thought I had seen the depths of poverty when I visited Haiti once, but that was before I stepped out of a C-130 at Chagh-charan.

Being at a NATO base, I found myself working alongside people from Lithuania, Croatia, Denmark, Iceland, plus a handful of countries I had never heard of or knew existed. The land and surrounding area was so desolate I felt like I had landed on the other side of the moon.

It was a far cry from my cozy office I had left back in Michigan.

Chapter Three
Why Overseas Contractors Exist

What is a contract worker? Most people think of a contract worker as being like someone you hire to put on a roof or some other type of construction work. Or they think of contract workers as someone who works for a company from their home making a software program or something similar and then deliver a final product to a company for payment. Contract workers in the States are generally people who are not on the company payroll. They may work on specific projects within a company, but they are not viewed or paid as permanent employees.

The contract worker I'm talking about is someone who does military contract work or other government-type work overseas. We work for one of several companies, getting paid regularly, getting benefits, etc. The term "contract worker" comes about because we're not expecting to spend a lifetime working the job. We usually sign a one-year contract at a time. Plus, the projects we are working on exist usually because of contracts a company signs with the US Government.

It simply comes down to economics. The military has discovered that it fights very well, but it has also discovered that using soldiers for KP (Kitchen Patrol) duty is not the most efficient use of their training. Since they never know how long a war, conflict, or natural disaster will last, why should they keep thousands of troops on standby to peel potatoes for years at a time for no reason?

Also, there is a term called "legacy cost." This is the cost incurred when someone serves in the military for a few years and then the military continues to be responsible for their costs years after that person has left. These costs could be education benefits, retirement, disability, etc. As a military contractor, all you get is your pay. That's it. Once you leave the contracting world, the US military has no long-term financial obligation.

There are other civilian type contract jobs through US AID and other government agencies. You might be building bridges or repairing power plants or showing farmers how to irrigate or get higher crop yield. But with those contracts you would not be operating from a. base or a compound. You would be living with the people you are serving. This means living in local housing, eating food from local gardens, and struggling through power outages several times a day.

Chapter Four

Soldiers Come First

If you work with the military, this is an axiom that all military contract workers live by. You are there to support the soldier. That means if the showers used by soldiers and the showers used by contractors are broken at the same time, the soldiers' showers are fixed first. I have heard occasional complaints from soldiers who thought we took care of ourselves first. There might be some very rare isolated cases that may have happened, but I know that 99.9% of the time we always sacrificed to make sure the soldier was taken care of first whether they realized it or not. We also work countless and sometimes unpaid hours to make sure the soldiers are taken care of.

Here's an example of contract workers I've worked with going the extra mile to care for the soldiers. It was at a base where we had set hours at the dining facility.

It was about five minutes to closing time. We knew one of our patrols had come under attack and was limping in with damaged vehicles. We had confirmation no one had been seriously hurt but these were "our" guys and we were concerned. Over my communication line that all the managers used, the Commander of the base came on the radio and was asking me if there was any way the Dining Facility could stay open a little longer so these guys could get fed. Before I could respond or even ask our Dining Facility manager about what we could do, he came on the radio "The lights in the dining facility will NOT go out until those guys are fed."

A few hours later those men sat down to a warm meal. I heard not one complaint from my guys who had to work late that night.

Chapter Five

What Are These "Contracts?"

Every company and every contract is different. The biggest contract right now is called LOGCAP (Logistics Civil Augmentation Program), but there are others that exist. KBR (Kellogg, Brown, and Root) is famous for being the largest employer for the longest time under the LOGCAP contract. In recent years the military has broken up the LOGCAP contract into smaller pieces.

Typically a job would work like this. You would sign a one year contract. This is not the military; you can quit at any time. But there are usually financial incentives for finishing a contract and penalties for not completing it.

Most jobs are broken into two different work types. Some are 12 hours a day 7 days a week. It is hard but you usually get into a routine.

The other common contract I've seen is 10 hours a

day 6 days a week. Since you are paid on an hourly basis the money can add up fast working 84 hours a week. On top of your hourly rate you usually also get paid "uplift." Uplift is basically your danger pay for working in a war zone. I've seen people get 35% up to 80% uplift on their pay per hour. Sometimes it is paid over all your hours or just on the first 40 hours worked.

Most companies will give a sign-on bonus of a few thousand dollars (Ballpark: $2,500 to $5,000) as well as a completion bonus for completing your contract (Ballpark: $2,500 to $5,000).

All contracts have an R&R or Rest and Relaxation system. This is your vacation time. Usually you will get some vacation time after working 90, 120, or 180 days. In my opinion, the ones that only give R&R every six months are the toughest, especially if you have a family.

How you pay to go home depends on the company. Some give you an allowance to buy your own ticket home and if you can find a cheap ticket you get to keep the difference. Others simply buy your ticket to where you want to go. Also, most companies will pay for your ticket home if you complete your contract.

If you do not complete your contract, I've seen companies take back the sign-on bonus, charge you for mobilization cost and your ticket home. You can see there is a definite incentive to complete your contract.

As long as the jobs exist I've seen guys complete their contracts, take a few months off, reapply and get hired. Sure, they'll start back at the bottom of the seniority pole and they may not be able to go back to the place they used to work, but the pay is still outstanding. My favorite example of this was when I had a worker who was a soccer nut. He had completed his one year contract and went home for no other reason than to watch the world cup tournament. Now by pure luck, we had an opening at the same time he decided to reapply so we were able to rehire him and it was like he never left. This was a lucky thing for him because that doesn't always happen.

C h a p t e r   S i x

How To Find A Contract Job

There are three main ways you can find a contracting job.

1. The Internet.

2. Through contacts with someone already working overseas.

3. Job Fairs.

Below is a partial list of companies' websites that have opportunities to work as an overseas contractor

www.exelisinc.com

www.bv.com

www.kbr.com

www.fluor.com

www.thefourhorsemeninternational.com

www.leoniegroup.com

www.contrack.com

www.battelle.com

www.usaid.com

www.louisberger.com

www.advantagetr.co.uk

www.atcosl.com

www.aecom.com

www.metechservices.com

www.stsii.net

www.l-3com.com

www.altegrity.com

www.baesystems.com

www.dfsmiddleeast.com

www.qinetiq-na.com

www.paegroup.com

www.iapworldwideservices.com

www.dyn-intl.com

www.lockheedmartin.com

This is by no means a complete list. Contracts come and go every day. They may or may not have jobs on the day you are looking so keep checking their websites to see about openings.

Obviously, having friends over here helps. If a person brings in a resume to me and will stake their reputation that you would be a good worker, that is a definite plus in my book. I love referrals from existing employees. However, if this person is a poor performer, it might hurt you. So if they are an "idiot" friend, you probably should not ask them to take your resume to Human Resources.

Make sure you keep up with your friend trying to help you get a job on Facebook and LinkedIn. Don't bug them every day, but checking in every so often does not hurt.

Some companies will hold job fairs around the country. If you have a chance to go, do it! If we get to see you face to face, the odds of you getting a job increases greatly.

Remember: most expenses associated with a job search such as gas and hotel are usually tax deductible. Keep records and receipts.

If you do make contact with an HR professional or a recruiter, go ahead and contact them every few weeks. Repeat with me, "every few weeks."

Some people contact me every day. That does not impress me. In fact, it bugs the heck out of me. But a reminder every so often does not hurt and lets us know you're still interested and serious about finding work.

Chapter Seven

Applying For A Job

As a Human Resource professional I have gotten thousands upon thousands of emails, phone calls, and letters applying for a job. I will now let you know how NOT to apply for a job.

1) Do not . . . I repeat . . . DO NOT open with statements like "I'm going to lose my house, I need the money, I'm going to go bankrupt, etc." Not to sound mean, but we don't care. If you were rich you would not be applying for a job! We all have bills to pay and other financial goals. Opening with statements of desperation is unprofessional and just signals us you will probably add an element of drama to our project. Something we do not need.

2) Do not apply for every job that is listed. I've had people apply to be firefighters, food service workers, HR professionals, project managers, and laundry work-

ers, all with the same resume and on the same day. I find it funny they seem to think we will "accidentally" hire them. No one has qualifications to do every job a company has to offer. In my opinion, people who do this lack serious judgment and therefore are not people I want on my team.

3) When applying, make it simple for the HR person to qualify you for a job. S/he can have 3,000 or more people apply for the same job. Having a long resume with no guts to it takes up too much time. I always appreciate people who make it easy for me with cover letters or emails that basically say something along the lines of: "You require this, this, and this, I qualify by having that, that, and that." It makes it easier for the HR person to review and forward your application to the hiring manager for consideration.

One more tip: If you are serious about applying for a contractor job, make sure you have all the certificates and licenses you need. If you need to finish something up in order to receive a license or need additional training, hurry up and get it. You don't know when the call might come, and once you're hired—as in my case—you're expected to be able to show up fast.

I once worked on a project that needed fire fighters. I had no problem getting fire fighters stateside to apply, but a lot of them did not have a particular Airfield certification. It would only have taken them about two weeks of part-time work to finish getting that certification. We had to turn away hundreds of applicants because they did not have it. Taking the time to better yourself with schooling is important for any job - not just overseas contract work.

Chapter Eight

The Interview

You have to be flexible if you get lucky enough to get contacted for an interview. You are dealing with so many different time zones you may have to interview at 2:00 a.m. your time. You would be surprised how many people will NOT give me a phone interview on a Saturday. For no particular reason. Guessed when I call them a second time? Never.

In the interview, please just be honest. We don't expect you to know everything or understand every term we use. For example I might interview a food service worker and ask them if they have ever worked in a DFAC before. Someone who has worked stateside does not have a clue of what I'm saying and since I use that term a hundred times a day I forget to use other terminology. DFAC simply means Dining Facility or at stateside we would say "cafeteria." It's okay to say, "I'm not familiar with that term." The HR person will kick themselves for forgetting you may not know all our terms. They'll explain it and then give you a chance to respond. That is so much better than trying to pretend you know what we're talking about when you don't.

The interview is pretty much like any interview you would have stateside. You could have three people calling at the same time to interview you. Remember that sometimes these people are calling from tents in the middle of nowhere and communications is a struggle. If you get cut off three or four times, don't become frustrated. Just be patient and roll with it. It isn't their fault. They are not deliberately trying to annoy you.

Patience is the key to succeeding over here, so if you start acting impatient with my sometimes faulty communications gear, I know you are going to be impatient when you get here - and I don't need that on my project. Interview over.

There are many books on how to interview and I suggest you read a few and practice interviews with friends and family. I've had people say to me, "I haven't had to interview for a job in years. I should not have to bother with this." So they did not agree to interview with me. Guess what? They also did not get hired. There are legal reasons why we have to do interviews, so just get over yourself and go with it.

Usually you will be asked two basic types of interview questions. The first is behavioral. They will be questions like "Tell me about a time you really messed up." I can't tell you how many people use examples like "I just worked too hard," or "I'm too hard on myself with deadlines." Blah blah blah.

Here's what I'm looking for: I can tell the bigger the mess-up you admit to lets me know you are honest. Then, more importantly, tell me what you learned from it and how you fixed your mistake. It's that sort of information that will make me take you seriously. No one is perfect and we know that. If you are not failing every so often, that means you are not taking chances, which in my book translates into lack of effort and initiative on your part.

The second type of questions you will typically be asked are technical in nature. This is where I sometimes get lost as an HR professional. At that point, the hiring manager becomes very important. If, for example, you are being interviewed for an IT (Information Technology) position, then you will be asked those types of technical questions.

Just like stateside, you might have to interview two, three, or more times. Again, it just depends on the different companies' internal systems. Roll with it and make yourself available to interview at a moment's notice.

Chapter Nine

Offer Letter, Paperwork, Etc.

When you get an offer letter, just know that you are now going to have to do lots of paperwork and fill out all sorts of documents.

First of all, if you do not have a passport, go get one now!

Yes, now.

I'm not kidding. It can take several weeks to get it. I cannot tell you how frustrated I have gotten waiting on someone to get a passport. Everyone should have one anyway. Plus, while you're at it, go ahead and get your whole immediate family their passport. You will most likely be meeting them out of country for a vacation at some point during your contract.

Details on getting a passport: You will have to get two passport photos for yourself. If you happen to be an AAA member they will do a set for you for free. (At least my local AAA office does.) It will cost about $135 for a brand new passport. If you already have one, the fee is a little less to renew at around $110. You will want about 6 blank pages for country stamps. Every time you land in Dubai or Iraq, they will stamp your passport. Every time you land in the US, they will stamp your passport. Plus, if you are working in Afghanistan or Iraq you may need a work visa. As you can see the pages can get used up pretty fast. If for some reason you are running short on pages, you can get pages added.

Get all your other documents in one place. Birth Certificates, School Diplomas, Certifications, Licenses (Such as electrical or plumbing,), even tax returns. You never know which document will give you the data you need to fill out the paperwork and it is better to do it NOW so when you get that offer letter you can very quickly fill out all the other paperwork that comes along with it. You'll be stressed out enough once you get that offer letter. No need to add to the stress when a few hours of work now will take care of things.

Below is the link to the US State Department's website to print off needed documents, instructions and fees.

http://travel.state.gov/passport/

Most companies are trying to fill the positions they have as quickly as possible. There are financial reasons for this plus they want to make sure the soldier is taken care of.

A distracted soldier is a dead soldier. As an HR professional helping to fill contracting jobs, I want to make sure the soldiers can concentrate on their jobs. If they can not get good rest and are not alert on patrols, then it is my fault.

Therefore, what some companies will do will give out multiple offer letters for one position. The first candidate to finish with all the paperwork, pass a security check and a physical usually gets the job. The others will have their offer "pulled" or put into a holding pattern until another position opens, if ever.

That is why I'm telling you that if you are serious about applying for a contract job, it is so important to get your documents ready to go. IT WILL GIVE YOU A LEG UP ON THE COMPETITION.

Chapter Ten

Security Check

Hopefully by this point you will have been given an offer letter. Usually it will be contingent on whether or not you can obtain a security clearance. There are several different types but the main three are:

1. Trusted Person or NACI clearance,

2. Secret

3. Top Secret.

I'm telling you right now it is a pain to fill out all the paperwork to apply for whatever clearance the job requires. It will ask you for about 10 years of data. You have to supply it all. It took me forever to figure out an old apartment address where I had briefly lived in that time frame.

The most important thing I can tell you about the clearance application process is DO NOT LIE or LEAVE SOMETHING OFF thinking the investigators won't find out about a black mark in your past! The Government Agencies involved in investigating the individual know everyone is not perfect.

If you had a criminal past, disclose it. If you had some bad debt or bankruptcy, disclose it. The Government Agency may ask to interview you and ask you specific questions about that part of your history. Again, just be honest. The investigators know what they are doing and you are not going to dodge their investigation by lying.

The companies doing the hiring do not know why someone passes or not. They are simply told whether or not a potential employee has passed or failed by whichever Government Agency has conducted the investigation. However, I have had enough people tell me about their issues that I can usually figure things out. For example, one candidate recently told me that less than a year ago he had declared bankruptcy and he had disclosed it. He had to give an interview to the government official and he explained all the reasons for his bankruptcy. A few weeks later he got his clearance and was working for me.

I had another worker fail his security clearance check. He was furious. It turns out he had an unpaid bill to a dentist for around $800 from years before. He owed this debt and ignored it. It wasn't until he knew he had to apply for a clearance that he called the dentist office and set up a $50 a month payment plan. If he had been unemployed or just starting a new job I could understand his actions maybe, but it turned out he had been working a $100,000 job for the past 16 months and never tried even once to make good on his legitimate bill. He failed his clearance and I had to terminate him. He had demonstrated he could not be trusted and did not make a good faith effort to keep his word and pay his bills. The government is not going to trust anyone like this with classified information.

One time for my clearance I was contacted by a government agency saying they needed to interview me. The gentleman was very nice; he met me at the hotel lobby where I was staying, and we went and got a cup of coffee in the hotel restaurant. He showed me his identification, looked at my passport, swore me under oath to tell the truth, and proceeded to ask me identity questions. It turns out my name was similar to someone else's on a "bad guy watch list." He just had to verify I was not that guy. We ended up having a very pleasant conversation for forty five minutes.

Now don't think if you get a clearance you are going to get access to all our country's secrets. You are not going to find out who shot JFK, gain access to Area 51, or be given the formula to Coca Cola. Our military just needs to know you know how to keep your mouth shut about troop movements, expansion/shutdown plans of bases, etc. Having security clearance is not all that glamorous, but it is sometimes very important when it comes to getting a contract job.

Chapter Eleven

Medical

Almost all companies require a medical/dental exam before you come over. At the time of the writing of this book the military is requiring you to pass what they call a MOD 11 medical which is very difficult to pass. I won't go into all the details of what is required of the MOD 11 but I'll hit on the highlights. One thing I will recommend is find your shot records. If you have no record, you will get every shot needed for the area you are going to. I know guys who have been vaccinated 3 or 4 times for Hepatitis A&B because they lost their records.

The most common reason I know for people getting bumped is for Diabetes, BMI (Body Mass Index) of 40% or more, heart conditions, etc. For all the details, just do a search of MOD 11 on the internet and you can see if you think your own medical conditions might knock you out.

If you are going to start applying for contracting jobs and have medical/dental issues, work on them now. I made sure I went to the dentist when I started the process and I deliberately lost a few pounds. It may require you to use some vacation time on your current job, or weekend appointments. Hit the treadmill, track, elliptical, etc!

Most companies use a national company to conduct these exams. Turns out the closest clinic they could send me to was a 2 hour drive away even though I had a state-of-the-art occupational health clinic 20 minutes from my house. I had no choice and I had to make that drive. It was a terrible clinic. It took me a while to pass. They kept writing down the wrong information on me. Somehow they made me 5 inches shorter than I am and added 60 pounds of weight, so I failed the BMI. I had to go to the doctor again to get certified that I was below the 40% BMI. It was a pain but patience is the key to succeeding in this particular work environment.

One of the most popular questions I get asked from candidates is why is the BMI so important on the medical? Well, besides the obvious heart attack risk and other medical issues, it comes down to extraction. If you get wounded or killed, and have to be dragged to a Med-Evac chopper or another vehicle while under attack, other people will be having to carry you. These people are already risking their lives, have on their own body armor, weapons, ammo, etc. and now they are trying to save your rear end. If you are obese, with body armor, plus other gear you might have on you, they could be dragging 300 or 400 pounds of dead weight. That's too much for anybody to drag to a helicopter and load. So people that fit that profile are not hired for contract positions.

There are, however, some programs that do not require a medical. I have never understood this. Another HR Manager worked a few doors down from me for another company. One day I saw one of her employees walk out. He was huge. Not just big, Huge.

I quietly asked the other HR manager, "How in the world did he pass his medical?"

She responded, "We are not required to issue one for our program."

My jaw dropped and I asked, "If he gets wounded, how are you supposed to drag him to a secondary vehicle while your Personal Security Detail team are fighting to protect you?"

She said, "We never thought of that."

So my point is there are some companies that might hire you even if you are obese, but if things heat up on some foreign soil and you need to be extracted, you will be putting your life and everyone else's life in danger around you.

I'm not talking from a standpoint of a skinny person who has never had to worry about their weight. I try to get up at five a.m. and work out for a thirty minute to full hour every morning before I go to work in order to fight my own weight battle. I'm not always successful! Do I want to work out at five every morning? No. But after five years over here, I know exactly how fast things can go wrong, and what it feels like to have to scramble for the bunkers when mortars start exploding. Being relatively lean and strong makes that scramble go a whole lot faster. It also keeps me in good enough shape that I can help drag someone else to safety if they get wounded. One joke we always say, "If the Taliban come over the wall, I don't have to be the fastest runner, I just have to be faster than you!"

You may be required to take Malaria prevention medication. Some companies require you to take it no matter where you are in the country. They are just trying to cover themselves but it does get ridiculous at times. One base where I worked was high on a mountain and we got a wind chill of minus 60 degrees. We had to keep our trucks running all night because they would be frozen by morning. Mosquitoes, the primary carrier of the malaria bug, are not a problem where it's 60 below.

However, we took our malaria medication. The official line was "Take the medication."

I would suggest you talk to your doctor first before you take any medical advice from me. I made the personal decision of not taking the medication during winter months or only if I was in an area with mosquitoes. My own personal doctor said it was not good to take the medication every day for years at a time. Again, check with your own medical professional!

If you get sick while over here you normally have two choices for treatment. First will be the private clinics that will be on most bases. They can take care of the basics. Cuts, colds, etc. If it requires more advanced care you will always have access to Military Medical facilities. Most often though, they will not see you first, so you usually have to go through your company directed clinic on site. Some doctors are great, others not so. I recommend you have a good relationship with your doctors back home. Try to get in with them during periods of R&R and take care of yourself as much as you can then.

By the way, I always bring back gifts for the doctors and their staff when I visit stateside for check-ups and such. It might be dates from Dubai or cloth book marks made by a local Afghan womens' group. Just a little something to say thank-you.

I always try to pre-plan my stateside doctor visits but it does not always work out with flight delays, etc. Very rarely do I have a problem with the staff getting me in for a last minute appointment or rescheduling. Mainly that is because they know what I do for a living and understand the position I am in—but I don't think it hurts that the staff usually knows I'm bringing something exotic from the Middle East for them. However, I do not bring the gifts just for the flexibility: I truly appreciate everything they do. More than once my dentist has had to stay late to fix a dental problem, or during annual medical time, my cardiologist's staff had to squeeze me in for tests and such.

# Chapter Twelve

Training

Almost everyone will have to go through a week long class called CRC (CONUS Replacement Center). They are held at various locations throughout the US Basically it is designed to tell you what to expect when you are coming over, to verify your medical results and immunizations, and to go over lots of safety stuff. The company will usually provide your transportation there and you will sleep in a tent eating leftover MRE's (Meals Ready to Eat). This training is not interesting, mostly rules and regulations. It is mostly PowerPoint presentations and pretty boring but it is required and you just smile and check off the needed boxes.

Don't be a jerk or mouth off to anyone because they will have the power to send you home. Just remember the people doing the training are just doing their jobs. A lot of it is waiting on others to get their missing immunizations or waiting on the next speaker to show up. Don't get me wrong, you will learn some things. My favorite written question was "You see a land mine. Do you (A) step on it, (B) Ignore it or (C) Report it to the nearest soldier."

Chapter Thirteen

Safety

A lot of the training focuses on safety issues. I cannot stress enough how important the safety is. From keeping dust out of your eyes, to reporting a strange package, to rockets coming in. My favorite quote when it comes to safety is "Better to be laughed at by thousands than carried out by six."

One night I was just leaving the showers and was walking back to my cot when BOOM, a rocket came in. I hit the ground and just laid there as flat as I could. About that time a few soldiers came running out of the building I was lying next to. I was in my Crocs, t-shirt and shorts with my towel and toiletry bag flung on the ground next to me. Here they come running out looking like multiple Rambos with their guns, body armor, etc. They stopped when they saw me.

"You okay?" One of the soldiers asked. It was too

dark for me to see his rank.

I replied, "Just kissing the ground 'till the all clear, sir."

"Good job," he said, and then he ran toward the wall surrounding the base with fighting positions at the ready.

Did I look stupid? Sure I did, but not so stupid when that second rocket came in and landed nearby. If I had been Joe Cool and just stood there, shrapnel could have taken my head off. When the all clear sounded I simply walked back to the showers because I was covered in dust from lying on the ground.

False bravado is not a characteristic the military appreciates or needs out of contract workers. They would much rather the civilians working with them use some common sense and stay out of the way while the soldiers do the job they're trained for—which includes protecting civilians.

# Chapter Fourteen

What To Pack

Some lists I've seen companies recommend are way overkill. You just need the basics and then once you get to where you are going permanently, you can always have it mailed over. I discuss mail later but you can get other supplies usually in 7 to 10 days. Based on my experience, what I recommend you pack is:

About 3 pairs of pants, 5 shirts, 7 pairs of socks and underwear, travel sized toiletries, some bedding such as a sheet and small pillow, shower shoes, towel, and depending on time of year, winter clothes (coat, hat, and gloves). You can get anything basic you need at the PX. Also, pack a pair of shorts and 1 or 2 t-shirts to go back and forth to the bathroom.

If you need prescription medication, bring a 90 day supply. This item is especially important.

I was so stupid coming over the first time. I had

made sure I packed everything on the formal list I had been given. My luggage was extremely heavy! I was ready for the zombie apocalypse with all the clothes, medications, hand warmers, etc. It was such a pain lugging that stuff from one base to another. By the way, don't expect to get any help carrying your luggage. You are going to carry it no matter what. Everyone else is carrying their own stuff and they don't have extra arms. It does not matter if you are a man or a woman; you carry your own load.

Another item you will want to bring is a head lamp. These are flashlights with elastic on them to wear around your head. It frees up your hands to pack or look for other items in the dark. It doesn't sound like a big deal but on a bunk bed in the middle of the night you don't want a flashlight beam flying all over the place as you try to fumble around, holding it with your teeth or armpit, while you try to search for something.

Chapter Fifteen

Type Of Clothing To Bring

Now this is purely a personal preference but my favorite clothing to wear over here is a brand named 5.11. You can almost always tell a "contractor" because this is the clothing of choice. The clothing is tough, durable, dries fast and is made for this climate. It keeps you cool in the summer and warm in the winter. It lasts forever.

My family made a little bit of fun over the fact that I even preferred wearing it when I was home with them. That was before my family and I were vacationing together in Grenada during R&R. After we had done laundry, my wife could not believe how quickly my clothing dried, in comparison to everyone else's as it hung outside to dry. She said she guessed she would have to stop making fun of it after all.

The 5.11 clothing has pockets all over them so you can store a lot on your body. This is really handy if you are moving around a lot through the day to various locations. You can get this clothing just about anywhere online but my favorite website to purchase it through is www.lapolicegear.com because they'll ship to military addresses. Plus, they almost always have a 5.11 Close-out section and I check it about once a week to see if something I need/want is on there. And no, I do not receive a discount or any freebies for putting this clothing line or website in my book!

Chapter Sixteen

Living Conditions

Living spaces are usually given out based upon job position and length of time "in theater." ("In theater" refers to the general area of military operations.) There are three basic types of living quarters.

1. The first is tents. Tents are usually cramped and open. I once stayed for months in a tent built to hold 100 people and we had 300 in there. We nick-named it the "infirmary" because one person would get sick and all of us would have whatever was going around. Also, there are many nationalities crammed in a tent with different safety and hygiene standards. Theft is also usually a problem. You always want to try and lock up your valuables. It's frustrating. One time I left some hair gel on my bed and someone stole it. It was frustrating because if they had asked, I would have given them the whole bottle. (I found if you ever needed anything, you

could just stand in the walkway between the bunk beds and say "Hey, anyone have any extra soap they don't need?" Whenever anyone did this someone always had extra of whatever they needed.)

2. The second type of living quarters are what they call B-huts. They are small buildings built of plywood. Usually they are painted with a little gasoline to help keep the bugs out of the wood. These buildings are broken into rooms of 8 or 10. You always hope to get an eight man B-hut because you actually have a little room. With a 10 man B-hut you have just enough room for a cot or single bed and to stand up and change clothes. But at least it is private and theft is a little less of a threat in a B-hut since you can actually shut and padlock a door. However, they are cold in the winter and hot in the summer. There's little climate control in these living quarters. A fan is allowed for summer but space heaters are usually prohibited because of the fire hazard they pose.

3. The third type of living quarters are called "containers." These are usually modified shipping containers. This is usually the most luxurious of living conditions you can expect. Sometimes you will get one all to yourself but I've seen others that are bigger and they put in bunk beds. If you are really, really lucky you might get a "wet container." These are containers that actually

have a bathroom in them.

Speaking of bathrooms… you will almost always have to walk to showers and bathrooms. It is miserable in the dead of winter to walk through cold snow and mud to get to one of them. You are always wide awake by the time you get back to your bed. It might not have been all that healthy to do this, but I would avoid drinking water in the evening just so I would not have to get up in the night to go to the bathroom.

Showers are always a challenge. First, depending on the time of day, good luck getting a hot shower. Second you will be in showers being used by people whose cleanliness standards are considerably lower than yours. A good pair of shower shoes is absolutely essential. Unfortunately, I have seen where people have actually pooped in shower stalls. I never could tell if it was a culture thing or just being mean, but seeing a "Baby Ruth" lying there on the floor made me gag more than once.

Plus, some contractor workers come from very poor countries. We had built brand new state of the art showers. They were so nice. Several days later someone had stolen all the shower heads. We found out they had been stolen by some non US citizens and they were renting the shower heads to their own countrymen! It was frustrating but sad at the same time.

# Chapter Seventeen

Sleep

Sleep is your lifeblood. If you are not getting it, you are going to have a personality change. Period.

It is hard to get enough sleep, especially when you first land. You are in a different time zone and odds are you are hearing jets and helicopters take off all night long. Bring some good ear plugs and eye shades. The lights in the temporary living quarters you will be in before you get your permanent quarters will be going on and off all night long. Some people have no respect for others trying to get sleep. Plus others will be leaving to catch flights all night long and they will be making noise packing and dragging their luggage out into the night. More than once I have sent people home because they started fighting and I'm sure it was due to just pure exhaustion.

Your comfort as you sleep is not a priority for your

company. One of the worst places I have slept in is a tent with bunk beds. Some "genius" decided that it would be a good idea to make a "Y" with the bunk beds. Meaning 3 sets of bunk beds were connected. We were not sleeping side by side but about two feet of the beds were bolted together so when one of the six people sleeping rolled over it shook the other 5 people.

When you are sleeping in bunk beds, getting a bottom bunk is the equivalent of getting the penthouse suite. When I was finally able to land a bottom bunk I built what I called a "fortress of solitude." I had seen many other do the same thing. They had felt blankets for sale in the PX for about $5.00. Two or three could surround your bed. It always amazed me to see the ingenuity some of the guys had in constructing their bottom bunks into private places. You can hang blankets down all around and make a little private space. It blocks out a lot of the light and muffles the noise a little. This may sound strange building these little fortresses of solitude but when you are working with people twelve hours a day, seven days a week, you just want to be by yourself.

Chapter Eighteen

General Order #1

There are many rules and regulations you have to follow. The company will have their own policy and procedures but there are the military rules as well. The main one is called General Order #1. This is a long document but the main thing you need to know about GO#1 is this: No Alcohol. No Drugs. No Porn. This is taken very seriously. You would be amazed at how many people lose their jobs over these three things. You are randomly searched when you come into the country. Plus, there are what is called Health and Welfare inspections. These inspections are just to make sure there are no fire hazards, vermin problems (mice and snakes), etc.

I am always amazed every time I'm a witness on these inspections. There is always someone who stupidly leaves evidence of violating this rule. Sometimes it is beer cans or porn DVDs just laying out on a desk. We photograph, make a statement, and then send the person home.

There are many foreign troops and foreign companies that do not observe General Order #1 and they are able to get in alcohol. I've sent more than one person home because they got alcohol through one of their foreign friends. People forget their alcohol tolerance level changes when they have not had it in months. They are used to being able to drink a case of beer back home, but because they have gone so long without it, their tolerance level goes down. So some get drunk on one beer and make a fool of themselves and show behaviors that let us know to test them for alcohol.

Here's my advice. If you can't live a few months without taking a drink, don't bother to come over. Just stay away and don't waste our time. As I had one camp manager once say, "If you have a beer I hope you enjoy it because that is a $100,000 beer you just drank." In other words, they would lose their job over it.

One time I helped bust a guy who was suspected of having child porn on his computer. I never saw it but the military monitors computer use and can take blown-up computers and piece them together. When this guy got reported to me, it was all I could do not to let certain people know. If I had, he would not have seen the sunrise. I did the right thing, kept my mouth shut, and followed proper channels. It was real interesting to have a US Federal Marshal show up to arrest him. I drove them down to the airstrip where the guy was put on the mail plane that came every few weeks.

On the next mail run the same pilot came back to drop off mail and asked me, "What the heck was with that guy and why didn't you warn me?"

I played dumb and said, "What are you talking about?"

He said, "As I was taxiing down the runway my plane was surrounded by MPs. They dragged that guy off the plane, threw him in the back of a truck and he was GONE."

There is an ending to this story. About a year later I was contacted by the US Attorney's office in Washington D.C. It took them awhile but the guy was thrown into federal prison. I'm a father of two kids whom I love very much. Frankly, I hope he rots in there.

Fighting is another violation of GO#1. You would think for a $100,000 job people could let things go. But there's always someone who says something idiotic and then the fight starts. I think it's a bit funny when people start making fun of each other's spouses, girlfriends, or boyfriends. Fights happen and then both people end up going home.

I once was talking about this issue with my wife

who said, "For a $100,000 job, they can talk all the smack about me they want. Don't you dare fight and lose your job."

So just remember: No one ever got fired from walking away from a fight. If you're here, and if you feel your temper starting to rise, just walk away.

Even if you are not caught by anyone violating GO#1, things can still go bad. More than once an employee has been found dead in his bed with a needle sticking out of his arm from a drug overdose. Over here drugs are cheap and easy to get. The big problem is you never, ever know what you are going to get. Sometimes that lack of knowledge can get you killed.

Chapter Nineteen

Eating

Eating is always an adventure. There are several eating options you have. Usually you will eat at a DFAC (Dining Facility.) Although the menu can get repetitive, you will get a square meal. You simply show your CAC (Common Access Card) or LOA (Letter of Authorization) and they will let you in. Most likely the soldiers get to eat in the first hour and then it will open up for contractors and other civilians.

Some bases have other eating choices such as a Burger King or Pizza Hut. You do not want to eat there every day but they do make a nice change for something different. Also, the DFAC usually has limited eating hours and the fast food places usually have longer hours. I always find it good to have tuna kits or oatmeal on hand when I don't want to go eat at the other dining places.

You always have to wash your hands and always take off your hat at the front entrance. You are not allowed to carry in backpacks or any other type of bag for fear of bombs.

When the no-bag rule went into effect, I had a general trying to walk in one time with a briefcase being carried by his aide. I understand how he must have felt. He probably needed that bag and didn't want to leave it outside where he couldn't keep an eye on it, but the top commander had said "No bags". My "lowly" DFAC worker would not let him in with that bag. The general's aide threw a fit. The worker kept pointing to the sign saying it applied to everyone.

I'm ashamed to say this general's aide soon came complaining to our base manager trying to get the DFAC worker fired. I loved this base manager. He listened to the aide complain for a few minutes then with a very serious face asked, "What was this worker's name again?"

The aide told him. The base manager said, "Thanks for letting me know. I'm going to give an award to that employee for following the rules that you all implemented. That rule, when it was issued by your superiors, did not say "No bags, except for generals.""

The aide's jaw dropped. We eventually did work out a solution with the general while he was visiting, but rules apply to everyone!

Chapter Twenty

Transportation

Transportation is one of the biggest headaches. First, there is getting into the country. Usually you will be flown to Dubai, Delhi, Kuwait City, or several other modern airports around the Middle East. You'll then board a private charter plane. Just because it is a charter plane don't be fooled into thinking it is a G7 or some other fancy plane. The planes I usually fly in are held together by duct tape and super glue. I always tell my wife the scariest part of being in a war zone is actually flying the charter in and out of Afghanistan.

Movement around the country can take several forms:

The military convoy. There are several ground vehicles you may ride in. First, there is the typical MRAP. You've seen pictures of those in the news. I will warn you, don't make the same mistake I did by not having your seat belt on and adjusted just right. The first time I rode one I was bouncing all over the place and my friend sitting next to me seemed to be just fine. Forty-five minutes later we pulled into the base we were traveling to and my rear end was sore.

We started to unload and my friend says "You were bouncing a lot."

"Yep," I said, "I must have been sitting over the wheel."

"Nope, you didn't have your seat belt on right," he replied.

I punched him in the arm and said, "Why didn't you tell me?"

He said, "The medic and I were laughing too hard at you."

It is dangerous traveling in these military convoys because they are visible from miles around. They have sirens going and guns pointing everywhere. It's wise to keep your eyes out the windows trying to help the soldiers you are riding with to watch for danger.

The second type of transportation is helicopter or airplane. You will get placed on a movement list. Since you are a contractor you are almost always behind soldiers who get the priority seats. Sometimes you will show up at 1:00 a.m. for a 4:00 a.m. flight, only to be bumped, and bumped again. You might wait 2 or 3 days for a flight out to where you need to go. Sometimes the waiting area is in a building or you might be sitting in a field. If you are lucky they might have bottled water and coffee. If you are unlucky, they won't. Always bring water or energy bars because you never know when and where you might get your next meal.

Just make sure you stay around the area so you can hear when they announce your flight. At a moment's notice they can call your flight and you gotta move fast.

The C130 is the most common airplane I've flown. There are other planes, of course, such as Russian-built planes, but it is always interesting to see what you will be flying in. Don't expect a nice stewardess and an in-flight movie and private bathroom. My biggest fear while flying in one of these is going to the bathroom. Sorry if this is too much information, but when you are flying in and out of the country on these planes, the need for a bathroom can get critical. Basically, all you have is a tube you can urinate out of. There is no provision made for any other bathroom needs. Because of that, I, along with others, usually take Imodium just to avoid that issue coming up.

You usually board the plane through the ramp that swings down from the back of the fuselage. Then you sit on uncomfortable fold-down seats, buckle in, and hang on for dear life. Now that I've flown in these things, it drives me crazy to watch Hollywood movies and see soldiers riding in the back of a C130 talking normally. Those planes are so noisy; you have to yell at each other to say a few words. Sometimes there is a mini white board you can write on and pass back and forth. Talking is just too much effort.

Sometimes you have to do a tactical landing which means that you do a tight spin, spiraling down to the landing strip. By doing this type of landing it gives the enemy less time to lock on with a rocket and try and shoot you down.

Helicopters are always my favorite way of getting around. It is straight up and straight down and not over roads where the bad guys like to plant bombs. Helicopters are much safer. You might fly in Black Hawks, Chinooks, or other types. You board, take the seat pointed out to you, strap in, and enjoy the flight.

Whenever you fly or convoy, you always want to check on the weight restrictions. I've seen newbies show up with everything including the kitchen sink and then try to cuss out a soldier for bumping them for having too much weight.

Chapter Twenty-One

OPSEC (Operational Security)

I cannot stress enough how important Operational Security is to everyone's safety. The main rule about Operational Security is to keep your mouth shut. Especially about movements. You are going to want to tell your family where/when you are going to different places.

Don't do it.

Wait until you are there. Then tell them you've arrived. The Taliban are not as technically backward as you might think. They monitor phone calls (Yes, even yours!) and you can inadvertently provide them with your itinerary.

Several times I've gotten on an aircraft and some idiot gets on his phone and says "We are lifting off now..." One time I slapped a phone out of a dude's hand. He decided to get all stupid with me but when ten other people yelled at him to sit back down he decided it wasn't worth it. It is very easy to lose your job if the military thinks you are breaking Operational Security. When in doubt, keep your mouth shut.

In fact, keep your mouth shut even when you aren't in doubt.

Also, I have seen people post some stupid pictures online. Sure the Taliban probably knows the basic layout of most bases but do you want to be "the guy" that posted a picture of yourself that gives the last bit of crucial information the bad guys need? Be very careful when you take pictures and upload them to the internet.

One time I wanted to take a picture of me holding a Happy Birthday sign for someone in front of an MRAP. There was a soldier sitting there on the MRAP and I asked him if I could take the picture.

He said, "I sure am glad you asked first. If you had taken that camera out and/or taken a picture I would have had to take you to the Military Police and you probably would have lost your camera. We are on a major picture lock down right now."

He was very nice about it, but he made his point. When in doubt, always ask if you can take a picture and when you do take some, don't post a bunch of them on your Facebook page.

# Chapter Twenty-Two

Preparing For Attacks

Now I won't go into a lot of detail about what to do during a rocket or ground attack. Obviously, I don't want the bad guys getting hold of this book and knowing our response plans. You will be briefed on this by your security manager at the location you are working.

One thing I will recommend is having a "bug-out" bag ready to go at any time. There actually is a name brand bag that is called a "Bug-Out" and I prefer their product for this purpose. The contents will change depending on the season, but basically you want to have a little food, water, a change of clothes, a small amount of needed medications, cash, your passport, and a coat, hat, and gloves if it's winter.

You will also want to make sure your phone is on your person at all times. You won't want to give your location, but you can let someone in your chain of command know you are unharmed.

This is again where I've seen idiots get on the phone and start saying their location. The bad guys can monitor phones, so again I must stress the importance of being careful. Attacks never come at convenient times. I've been in certain locations where people have been in their underwear and didn't have anything to cover up with. Thank goodness others had a jacket or something they could share.

Chapter Twenty-Three

Mail

One of the great things about contracting is the mail service you receive if you have access to an APO address. An APO stands for: Army Post Office. Unless you are at a very remote camp, you can usually get packages from the States in about ten to fourteen days for the cost of domestic mail. Your family can mail you all your missed items from home.

I find the best website to order stuff from is www.amazon.com. This is great for books, DVDs, etc. The only thing Amazon is not great on is shipping electronics such as laptops, iPods, etc. They usually will not ship these items to an APO.

For electronics I find www.tigerdirect.com to be the best. I've never had a problem with them shipping laptops, iPods, hard drives, etc.

For medicine (cold medication, aspirin, etc.) and

toiletries (shampoo, soap, etc.) www.drugstore.com is the best.

If you are missing any food items www.netgrocer. com is excellent. Every so often I needed some Peanut Butter Captain Crunch!

Just be sure not to have friends think they are doing you a favor by shipping things that don't belong or things that are illegal. The military does inspect packages and I've seen more than one person get in trouble because their buddies thought they needed beer, a playboy or drugs and tried to ship it over.

One thing that is always sweet is the care packages sent over for people trying to lift the spirits of troops over here. It was always cool to see a motorcycle club, church group, or some other organization send over care packages. The only problem is sometimes they send things not needed or things that will spoil quickly in the heat. One time we had a bunch of rice crispy treats show up. All were spoiled. So baked goods are not a good idea. You will also find sweet old ladies who remember WWII and will send over homemade mittens for the soldiers. Again, a wonderful idea just not practical in today's modern military supply system.

Post offices will only take cash or Eagle Cash cards. And a lot of times the post office will not have change so make sure you bring small bills to conduct your business. Mailing stuff out is a pain. The lines are long because every package has to be searched. No matter how many signs they put up, people are always trying to mail things not allowed. You would be surprised what can and cannot be mailed.

The list seems to change daily but some of the things that cannot be mailed out are batteries, any type of "war trophy" such as bullet casings, Afghan historical "treasures", any piece of a weapon such as sights or handles. Some people seem to think as long as it is not a weapon it can be mailed. If it can be attached to a weapon, it is not going to be allowed in the mail. They x-ray every piece that goes out. You may think you can pack it in a way to get through customs, but it will come back to haunt you. I know of one person who somehow was able to get about fifty bullet casings past the inspection. But a few minutes later it was x-rayed, found, and the person who was trying to mail it was sent home per military direction.

There are some ways of going through customs where you can mail knives and other items. So if you buy an antique gun from the bazaar (which is probably a fake) or a knife, go to customs first and have them inspect it and approve it to be mailed home. Then you go to the post office to mail the item.

One time I had had a knife given to me by a Nepalese friend. He was a bodyguard and I knew the knife was special. He explained to me the law of the knife. Anytime he unsheathes it, it has to draw blood, even if it is his own. My American buddy who was with me at the time confirmed this story with other Nepalese bodyguards in the compound.

I got to be friends with these Nepalese guards and one night, one of them told me, "You know as long as you stay here with us, I will let no harm come to you." Then he gave me his knife as a gift. I did not pull the knife out of the case in his presence. I did not want to accidentally trigger some bloody event. However, later on in private, I did take a good look at it and I treasure it.

So I went to customs, got the paperwork and mailed it home. It cost about thirty dollars to mail it, but it was worth it. Unfortunately, I forgot to tell my family I had mailed it home, so when they opened the box it was a bit of a shock to them!

Chapter Twenty-Four

Communications

When you are near bigger cities, communication is always easier. Cell phones are your life blood. Most countries that are rebuilding have learned going to cell service makes much more sense than trying to lay down land lines. I find that using a cell phone from the country you are in is cheaper. If you bring a stateside phone it can usually be used, but it is a lot more expensive. I always carry both. I use my local phone primarily to call home when I can not use Skype. I carry the stateside phone for extreme emergencies. My family can use that to get in touch with me just about anywhere at any time.

The other way to communicate with home is by Skype or some other VoIP (Voice over Internet Protocol) service. If the internet you use allows access, this is by far the cheapest and easiest. However, at certain times of the day the quality does suffer because everyone else is on it. At the time I write this Skype has a plan for $6.95 a month for unlimited calling to the States. It is a great deal. If you don't know how to use it, have some high school kid help you set up your account and show you how to use it. Most of them love showing off anyway.

Chapter Twenty-Five

R&R

When you are working 12 hours a day 7 days a week, sometimes the only thing that keeps you from going crazy is knowing your R&R (Rest and Relaxation) break is coming up. As I mentioned earlier, you may have R&R breaks at day 90, 120, or 180. Companies will give you an allowance or just pay for the airplane ticket you need. I always preferred the allowance because you usually can keep the difference. For example, a company may give you a $3000 allowance to purchase your ticket and take care of travel. If you can get a ticket to the states for $1500, you get to pocket the difference. This difference can go in the bank, help pay to fly your family to meet you somewhere, or just pay for a nice vacation.

Just like coming in to the country as a new hire you are usually flown through Dubai. Most companies will fly you charter from an airbase or you will fly commercial out of Kabul. What is neat about flying out of Dubai is you can visit places you never would have thought to before. For example, Cyprus was never a country I thought about visiting, but I spent a few days there touring the island and had a wonderful time. If you have a family, you could, for example, fly them to Paris or London and meet them there.

If you fly out of Kabul's commercial airport, you could fly straight to Turkey or India if you want a different adventure. I flew to India and spent a wonderful day there visiting. I was able to hire a driver, an air conditioned car, and an English-speaking tour guide for $50 for the whole day.

Some people always go home for R&R and others love to travel. There is no right or wrong way to do it.

Just make sure to take your R&R breaks. I have seen people purposely not take R&R just to save money. This is not healthy. You need a break. You cannot work 12 hours a day 7 days a week and keep your sanity. Even if it is a short break for Pepsi and nacho's in Dubai, take your break.

For instance, one time I had a worker in his 50s decide to start punching a kid in his 20s. Problem was the kid in his 20s lifted weights and was huge. The kid, of course, pounded him into the ground. When I was talking with the older individual I asked, "What in the world happened?"

He responded, "I don't know. He just said something that hacked me off and I started swinging."

This guy had never been in trouble before. I then asked, "When was the last time you had an R&R?"

He said, "Fourteen months ago."

No wonder he went crazy! However, since he got into a fight, he went home and the younger kid went home as well. Both were terminated for fighting.

One thing to be aware of, especially if you have kids and family, is jet lag. You can be traveling for over 24 or more hours depending on layovers. When you get home, hopefully your family is wild to see you. Your first few times of flying over it will be hard to adjust to the time change. The general rule is it takes one day for every one hour of time change.

I have developed a way to sleep on the plane as much as possible because it helps with jet lag. I make sure I stay up no matter what before the flight. No naps waiting on the flight! Once I'm on I take a few Tylenol PMs and try to sleep the whole way. Those economy class seats are uncomfortable, but you develop a tolerance for them. Those same seats always seem less tolerable when you are flying back to the Middle East.

One other thing if you have kids, be careful of "daddy or mommy guilt." You have been gone for months. You probably want to buy them the world to make up for it in iPods, computers, clothes, and other items. Be careful. You don't want them always expecting gifts. The main thing I did splurge on was trips. I feel it is important for kids to see the world. At the writing of this book, my kids have seen Canada, Bahamas, Grenada, and Mexico. Soon they will hopefully see Europe.

Chapter Twenty-Six

Financial Planning

For most people overseas contract work will produce the biggest paychecks they will ever see. I was a certified financial advisor for a few years. Unfortunately, I have seen many people get used to the big check, go home and try to live like they were still making 100 grand plus. They buy the big house, the big truck, jet-skis, motorcycles, ATVs, etc. They get themselves in financial trouble real quick.

Instead, I recommend you immediately try to get rid of all your debts before you commit to other financial obligations. Dave Ramsey is a financial planner that I highly recommend for you to read first even before you head overseas. He has a great plan of getting rid of debt and then building wealth. Check his book out of the library and put the money you would have spent buying his book to getting yourself out of debt.

First and foremost, if your company offers you a retirement plan such as a 401k, sign up as fast as you can and max out as much as you can. At the time of this writing, the typical 401k limit was about $17,000. If you are making $100,000 or more there is no reason you should not be maxing it out. Sign up even if the company does not offer a matching amount. I actually see people refuse to sign up because of lack of matching from the company out of "protest." They end up with nothing saved for retirement once they leave the project, and the company could care less.

You also may be able to sign up for an IRA for you and/or a spouse. Double check with your tax person or financial advisor.

Set up a second savings account for a part of your pay and have that money put into that account. I personally use an Ameriprise account. I purposely have it set up to where I can not immediately pull out money for a "want" instead of a "need." However, if something major comes up such as a blown transmission on my wife's car, she can write a check, and it will clear in two to three days.

Again, be careful with the money you make. I have seen people get more and more haphazard with how they handle their money. Some people will spend $5000 to $10,000 on business or first class tickets to go home.

To me that is just a complete waste. Typically I fly coach and round trip tickets to the States cost around $1500 to $2000. My plane seat arrives at exactly the same time as the business and first class seats!

Chapter Twenty-Seven

Life Insurance

As I've stated before, it is dangerous over here. There is the very real chance you could be killed. If you have bought a life insurance policy stateside, most likely it has a "war clause" in it. This means if you are killed in a war zone, they do not have to pay. Most companies offer company-sponsored life insurance through payroll deduction. All of them I've seen do not have the war clause in it, which means if you are killed, the insurance company will pay the beneficiary of your choosing. Most choices you have are buying $100,000 to $500,000 term policies.

One morbid joke I always tell my friends is, "If I get killed by a rocket, make sure my death certificate says I died of a heart attack before the rocket hit me so that my family will get both policies to pay out."

I find the rates for this type of insurance are comparable to the same prices in the States. In fact, I had bought a policy when my daughter was born. Ten years later I started contracting and signed up for the exact same amount as my stateside policy. The rates were almost identical even though I was ten years older.

If you have a family, max out how much you can get. If you are single and no obligations, still buy some. Your family has to bury you and those burial costs are never cheap.

Chapter Twenty-Eight

Short And Long Term
Disability Insurance

I once read a statistic that you are eight times more likely to need disability insurance than death insurance. Typically these insurances will continue a part of your pay if you have an injury or illness and cannot work. Most companies will offer some sort of payroll deducted company-sponsored plan. Again, I find the rates competitive to stateside rates with war clauses in them.

Short term insurance usually covers you for six months. If you continue to be unable to work, the long term insurance will kick in and last until you are qualified for social security or hopefully until you are healed.

Over and over again I see people try to save a few dollars and not elect it. As an HR professional I'm not supposed to endorse plans but I always try to get people to sign up. I have just seen too many people get hurt or suffer some illness and they end up going home with no pay.

I once had a worker in his mid-fifties arrive at my camp. I was briefing him on his benefits and strongly encouraged him to sign up for the disability insurance. It was only about $300 a year. According to him he was healthy as a horse and didn't need it. Three months later he gets a hernia. He has to fly home for surgery. It took him five month to recover and clear the military- mandated medical. Once he finally arrived back at my camp, he said he could not believe how stupid he was for not signing up and had no money during that time. I wish I could have made him a spokesman for insurance.

No matter what your age, you can always get hurt. Again, if you have a family and you do not sign up for this insurance, I think you are being irresponsible and not providing for them if something does happen.

Chapter Twenty-Nine

Taxes

Everyone thinks you make big, big money. The truth is if you worked two full time jobs stateside you can make about the same amount of money. Where you get ahead is the tax break. If you live outside the states 330 days per year you are usually exempt from paying federal and state taxes on about $95,100. Depending on your filing status that could be about $20,000 in your pocket instead of the government's.

To qualify for this tax exclusion you must be one of the following:

• A US citizen who is a bona fide resident of a foreign country or countries for an uninterrupted period that includes an entire tax year,

• A US resident alien who is a citizen or national of a country with which the United States has an income tax treaty in effect and who is a bona fide resident of a foreign country or countries for an uninterrupted period that includes an entire tax year, or

• A US citizen or a US resident alien who is physically present in a foreign country or countries for at least 330 full days during any period of 12 consecutive months.

To get more detailed information you can go to the I.R.S. website and search for foreign earned income exclusion.

Some states exempt you from paying state taxes while others do not.

Make sure you talk to your tax professional. Tax laws change all the time.

Chapter Thirty

Religious Activities

If you are a religious person, there are not a great many places to attend worship services. At your major bases they will typically have a chapel and different religions meet at different times. If you have access to this, it is a great way to meet new people and sometimes I've found the services help inspire me to get through another week. If you go to a smaller base, the odds of there being meetings will be less.

If you have a favorite preacher or inspirational speaker, I recommend getting the messages recorded before you leave home and put them on your computer so you can have your own service if nothing else is available. If you have a decent unblocked internet connection, then you may be able to download a weekly service from your place of worship. Don't try video, just try to download the audio. Video could take weeks to download.

# Chapter Thirty-One

Entertainment

Entertainment is always a big challenge. Typically bases will have a small or large MWR (Morale, Welfare, and Recreation). Usually they are reserved for soldiers but most will let contractors in. Some even have movies, ping pong tables, and even have popcorn from time to time. I find walking all the way down to where the entertainment was to be too time-consuming after a ten to twelve hour day.

Some places will have a gym. Again, it is usually reserved for soldiers, but most places will let you use the facilities if it is not full of soldiers.

I like to read books and watch TV. I recommend an eBook reader because when you start carrying your stuff from location to location, the weight of books really adds up. After a hard days' work, it is nice to lie on a cot and read a bit before falling to sleep. The best thing

I find for books is the Kindle Fire. Everywhere I go I'm able to download books on the Kindle. The Barnes and Noble Book Nook does not allow this for whatever reason.

As far as TV is concerned, I recommend a laptop or netbook. Download all you want while you are home because it is nearly impossible to download video in a harsh environment. It is easy to get DVDs. Most places have "bootleg" DVDs for sale around the bases and the PX will have legit DVDs for sale. It amazes me how a movie can open up in the US and a day or so later the local DVD shop will have it for sale. The quality usually is bad, but if you really want to see a movie or TV show the local bootleg shop will always have it. Even if you can download videos, they are usually blocked from "legit" sites, saying you are in the wrong region and will not let you download. All people will do is go buy illegal copies. I have no idea why movie and TV studios block being able to download over here—it just costs them money through lost sales.

Chapter Thirty-Two

Laundry

Getting laundry done is not a big challenge, but like all things here it requires patience. Basically, there are three ways laundry gets done. The most common way is you drop off your laundry at a drop off point. Most companies will supply a laundry bag. They may use a room number or an employee ID number on your bag as an identifier. Once your laundry is done they may post a list and then you claim your laundry. You will fill out an inventory list to go along with your laundry. At one time the local contract had a nine day turn-around time. You had to learn to be creative in how you timed everything.

The second most common way, if you are lucky, is to drop off your laundry outside of your living quarters and in the next day or so it will be delivered back to you.

The third way is a do-it-yourself laundry room. Some places have this. I've never found these easy. So many people are doing last minute laundry it can take hours and you will be waiting in a line. I've known people to get up at 3:00 a.m. to try and get it done and it still takes hours.

I've worked with all three options during my career. Don't count on whites to stay white. I've known people to wear white shirts only to see them go gray. I've never had a theft problem or laundry go missing. Sure there was the sock here or there but no major problems.

Just once did I have a problem. I was working at a compound and we came under heavy attack. A car bomb went off at the front gate and then several suicide bombers made their way into the compound. One of them ran into our laundry room. He was cornered and then detonated himself. His explosion destroyed a bunch of laundry, washers and dryers. No one was hurt in his explosion but my laundry was one of the casualties of the explosion.

A morbid joke we made about him is that in suicide bomber hell, he is the nerd of the bunch. His biggest claim to fame is that he made us go with dirty socks and underwear for about a week until we got in new washers and dryers.

By the way, as you can tell, when you work over

here, you get a pretty calloused sense of humor after a while. It helps you survive emotionally. It's wise to dial it down when you go home.

Chapter Thirty-Three

PX

The PX is where you purchase your items you *have to have now*. They claim to save you all this money but I never found their prices great. They are kind of like a 7-11. You pay for the convenience. It is feast or famine with what supplies they have. Sometimes they will have potato chips and then you can go months without seeing a bag. They also carry some electronics, DVDs, magazines, workout supplements, drinks, hangers, pillows, flashlights, etc. They will take cash, credit/debit cards, and Eagle Cash cards.

One thing different is they don't usually use regular coins. They use paper "pogs" instead. It cost so much to ship coins they use the pogs. They are actually kind of cool. They will have military pictures on them with the value of the pogs. In order to try and make sure everyone has a chance to purchase an item they will usually limit you to two of each item. Also, usually the first hour they are open is reserved for soldiers only.

Chapter Thirty-Four

Local Bazaar

Almost all bases and compounds have a "local" bazaar. It may be open once a week or seven days a week. This is where you can purchase jewelry, precious stones, bootleg DVDs, unlocked cell phones etc. Always haggle your price. Rule of thumb: you should only pay about half of what they are asking for.

Here are a few tricks I learned to make sure you do not get taken. First one of the most popular items to purchase is a stone called lapis. It is a beautiful blue stone. In fact the blue you see in Egyptian mummy cases and paintings are made out of this stone. At one time the stone was worth more than gold. Sometimes vendors try to pass off plastic as lapis. To make sure it is real, take a lighter with you. If it is real, it won't melt!

Another trick has to do with coins. It is amazing how many old US coins seem to be over here. Now some are real, but a lot of them are fakes from China. In order to have a chance of getting a real one, bring a magnet with you. Real coins are not magnetized. If the coins are fake, they will stick to the magnet.

It is best to build a relationship with certain vendors. If they are permanent, they actually have something to lose if they sell you something fake. Your legit ones will always make good on their deals. A friend of mine bought a precious stone. The vendor said the value would be X in the US If my friend had it appraised and it was not valued as the vendor said, he would give him his money back and pay for the appraisal. Well, it was appraised but it did not come to the value promised, and to his word the vendor gave my friend back his money and paid for the appraisal fee. The vendor made sure to make it right on my friend's next deal.

Chapter Thirty-Five

Banking/Credit Cards

I have never seen a US bank on base or any other compound. There are only two ways to do any sort of banking and get cash. The first is the military finance office if you are authorized to use it. They will issue you an Eagle Cash card, which is like a debit card. You will link up your Eagle Cash card with your bank account and put value on the card. If the card becomes lost or stolen, the military finance office will protect you. It seems that when the credit card machine is not working at the PX or at the local vendor shops, the Eagle Cash card will work.

Another option to get cash at your major bases and some compounds is a bank called Afghanistan International Bank (AIB) which might have a branch or ATM there. They usually limit you to $200 from the ATMs and charge you a $2.00 fee. I find most major banks have no problem going through their ATM. However, it seems Credit Union cards have the most problems being rejected. I personally have had no problem with the ATMs. One time I did try to pull out $200 and the receipt said I pulled out the money but no money came out. I emailed my bank all the information on the receipt and let them know no money came out. About two days later, the money was credited back to my bank account.

I've never had problems using my debit or credit card at the PX since its transactions are going through the US, but if you start traveling through different countries and plan to use your debit or credit card, make sure you call your bank or credit union and let them know. They will shut down your credit card so fast for fear of fraud/ID theft. You could use your credit card in 3 or four countries in less than 24 hours. I recommend having a separate card just for travel. More than once my poor wife had the debit or credit card shut down on her due to the bank putting me on fraud alert because I forgot to call them.

One way you may be able to send cash to someone is through Western Union which is usually available on the major bases. This is how most foreign nationals (Indians, Filipinos, etc.) wire money home. It is easy to use. You simply give the clerk your cash, the passport number of whoever is picking up the cash, a fee for the service and that money will soon be available to the designated person anywhere in the world where there is a Western Union office.

Chapter Thirty-Six

Global Entry And E-Gate

As I wrote earlier, you will fly a lot to/from the States and through Dubai. Two items I highly recommend you get is what I call quick entry cards. For the US they have what is called the Global Entry Card. You can find the details how to apply for it at this website.

www.globalentry.gov/howtoapply.html

Here are the basics. You become what they call a "trusted traveler" which means they've done a background check on you and know you are a trustworthy person. You do not have to wait in the passport line when you return to the US This may not sound like a big deal, but I've been in line two or more hours trying to get back in the States. If you have a tight connection for another flight you stand a real chance of missing your connection and the passport officials who work at these areas are not concerned about you making your connection. Their job is to protect the borders of the US. But it is frustrating waiting in that line. I recommend you get the card before you leave the US It costs $100. You have to fill out an online application, and you have to schedule an interview at one of the select locations throughout the US I got mine in the Atlanta International Terminal. You are still subject to random searches so don't be stupid!

Dubai has a similar card and it is a lot easier to get. It takes about 5 minutes. It is called an E-Gate card. It costs about 270 Dirhams which is about $73 US. They have a booth near the passport control gates. You go to the bank which is just across from where the booth is located. You give the 270 Dirhams to the bank and they give you a voucher. You take that voucher to the booth with your passport. They run your passport through a computer, if you pass their quick criminal check, they will take your picture and finger prints and then a minute later your E-Gate card will be handed to you. You pass through the E-Gate and out the door to your hotel if you are staying in Dubai for any time.

Dubai is another place where I have been in line over two hours waiting to get through passport control. The reason it takes so long is they have to do an iris scan on people from selected countries. It takes forever for them to get through the lines. Last time I went through Dubai I was out of the terminal in 15 minutes. The E-Gate card is definitely worth the expense if you are going to be making multiple trips through Dubai.

Chapter Thirty-Seven

Muslim Religion

I won't go into all the beliefs of Muslims and the history of the religion but there are a few things you need to know and be aware of. Muslims do not eat/touch pork. They really, really don't have a sense of humor about this. So don't make jokes about giving them bacon or ham. A few times I've seen a fight nearly break out when an expatriate would say as a joke he had let a Muslim eat pork.

One time at a remote base we were given an entire pig for a July 4th celebration. The locals were fascinated. They could not take their eyes off the pig as it was roasted but they refused to wash anything that had touched that pig. It was not US troops roasting the pig. We had Croatian soldiers there and they love to barbeque. So while we slept they stayed up all night cooking the pig.

Some Muslims will try to pray several times a day. I have not experience many Muslims that adhere to the five times a day routine. However, if you come across one in the middle of prayer, try to avoid walking in front of them. It is just rude because you are coming between them and Mecca.

The issue that is most difficult for me to deal with as a Human Resource professional is Ramadan. I once hired several local Afghanis to do some of the work on our base or in our compound. Almost all Afghanis are Muslim. When Ramadan came around my local workers observed Ramadan by not eating or drinking from sun up to sun down. It does not sound like a big deal but when you are working in 100 degree heat or hotter and not drinking water, bad things happen. More than once I have had a Muslim pass out from dehydration and crack his head on a rock or fall off a truck and end up hurt.

In order to accommodate Ramadan, we usually give extra breaks and longer breaks for those working outside. One time I had a group try to get an even longer break. The normal lunch break was 1 hour, but during Ramadan we gave them 1.5 hours. I got a call that there was a group demanding more time for prayer. I listened to them and to the "spokesman" for the group. It was obvious he was up to something.

I listened then asked, "You are strictly observing

Ramadan, correct?"

"Yes," he replied.

"Well," I responded, "if you are strictly observing Ramadan and not taking time to eat or drink you have 1.5 hours to pray, correct?"

That is when he started smiling.

I said, "I gotcha, didn't I?"

He responded, "Yes, but you can't blame us for trying."

I just walked away shaking my head.

In front of other Muslims, most will not take food or water. But if no one is looking a lot of them will sneak a snack or drink. When we started putting bottles of water around corners and other hidden places, it was amazing how many bottles disappeared and how all those workers passing out stopped!

Also, you may have heard the news about the Koran burning and the riots that happened because of it. Frankly, the local and international press got many of the facts of the story wrong. But, with that being said, don't burn a Koran, throw one away, or treat one with disrespect.

Chapter Thirty-Eight

Haircuts And Other Stuff

Almost every base or compound will have a place to get a haircut. Don't expect movie star quality. Usually the cost is about $8.00 for a basic cut. Some of the places not only give haircuts, but you can get massages, manicures, and pedicures.

I'm not sure why you would want all that done in a war zone, but if that is your thing, you have options!

Most of the workers do not speak fluent English so it may take a while to let them know what you want.

Chapter Thirty-Nine

Note For Those Back Home

If you have someone working one of these jobs it is hard to understand what they are going through. I think some people back home think they are having the time of their life. It is not fun. However, here are some things you should know and do. First of all, communication is a struggle. If you don't hear from them for a time, it is usually a communication problem. So when they get through, don't give them a hard time. Second, surprise them ever so often with a care package or card. I'm not necessarily talking about soap and shampoo but a treat they may not get for themselves. One of my favorite candies is See's Chocolate. It made my month when I once got some I was not expecting. Maybe it is a local BBQ sauce or some other regional thing. Just give them a "happy" every so often.

Bad news is not necessarily something that should

be shared over the phone. Yes, if someone has passed away or seriously sick and they need to come home that is one thing. But if your relationship is struggling, you want to break up, or get a divorce, don't do it in a letter or on the phone. Don't be a coward. Wait until they get home.

Way too many times my first responders had to show up to a contractor or soldier's quarters after they had gotten a Dear John letter. The person had committed suicide. The sound of that gunshot coming from the room and the people who rush in seeing the mess is something they will never forget.

They may not commit suicide, but a distracted soldier or contractor is a dead soldier or contractor. If people are upset, they may do something stupid or fail to see a threat they would have normally.

Also, your loved one does not want to stay in a war zone all their life. Live within your means and don't get spoiled with the income. I had a food service worker whose family got more and more dependent upon him. He ended up buying close to a million dollar home (this is before the real estate bubble) to house his whole family. He was not married but still had a lot of expenses. He went home for R&R and his family had fully furnished each of their rooms with a nice bedroom suit and big-screen TVs. His room was empty except for a mattress on the floor. I could not believe the disrespect shown him. Plus, now he is stuck over here forever to pay off that house and furniture.

So if you were not a designer person before your loved one went overseas, don't decide you have to become one. Keep your life simple. The job could end abruptly or worse, your loved one could be injured or killed and suddenly the money is gone. Live below your means.

Chapter Forty

No Green Grass On The
Other Side Of The Fence

With the "big" money comes more temptation to do stupid things. Middle-aged men will often think they are God's gift to women, be it prostitutes in Dubai or the sex trade in Thailand. I wish I could say it was a rare occurrence that a marriage fell apart while the spouse was "in theater." But when things are shaky at home, a trip to Thailand for R&R is a big temptation. Every time - I repeat, every time I have heard an employee talk about how he had found true love in Thailand, it has always ended badly. Now I'm not saying all Thai women are bad, but contractors need to remember the women they are seeing are not in love with them but with their wallet.

One of the worst examples of a contractor love affair I ever heard was with a contractor in his mid 50s. I'll change a little bit of the details to protect his identity but here is how the basic story went.

He was having some trouble with his wife of over twenty years. So instead of going home to work on his marriage he decides to go to Thailand. He meets a pretty girl in her early twenties and they "fall in love." He ends up divorcing his wife. He does not show up for the divorce proceedings so his wife gets everything. The house, savings, etc. He is even ordered to pay $80,000 in spousal support over the next three years. What does he care? He is making big money and he's traded in his old wife for something new.

Well, he decides to make a life with his new love almost 30 years younger than him. He buys a condo but since foreigners cannot own property in Thailand it is in his new girlfriend's name. He prepays about $16,000 for her to go to school and puts her name on the bank accounts. He heads back to work but instead of following the rules he get stone-cold drunk and misses his mandatory flight into Afghanistan so he gets terminated. He heads back to Thailand to spend some time with his new girl and to look for a new job.

After about two weeks she starts asking when he is going to return to work. He says he is not. So to take care of her little problem, she calls her brothers to come remove him. So as he is being drug out of "his" condo that was in her name by her brothers, she is calling the police to file "no trespassing charges" against him. While he is dealing with her brothers and police, she goes and cleans out the bank accounts and the prepaid tuition monies.

The story does not end there. A manager I worked with gets a strange phone call and the person placing the call says "You don't know me but I'm standing here with... and he has begged to use my phone to call you."

So my manager friend takes the call and hears the whole story about how he has lost everything. He has been wandering around the city for weeks begging for food and money. Imagine an American begging in Thailand. He called his ex-wife for help but she just hung up on him. So here he was begging for help.

My manager friend told him "You made your bed, now sleep in it," and hung up.

We found out later the guy who let him use his phone gave him enough taxi money to get to an embassy and got a micro-loan to buy a plane ticket home. After that I don't know what happened. Unfortunately, I have many more stories like these.

So here's my advice: Stick with the one you love, make the money to get out of debt, save and build a life.

Chapter Forty-One

Red Cross Messages

In the event of a crisis which requires an employee's presence at home, most companies will require an official "Red Cross Message." This is used to validate a true emergency. Communications have improved enough that most likely if there is a true emergency your family members will be able to contact you directly before the Red Cross message will be delivered. But in order for you to be approved for Emergency Leave a family member or close friend can call the Red Cross at 877-272-7337. The person calling will need to supply the following information:

Your Name

Company you are working for

Job Title and maybe Employee ID number

Social Security Number

Location

Nature of Emergency- Such as injury, death in family, etc.

The Red Cross will verify the information directly with the hospital or funeral home and then make the contact.

The Red Cross messaging service is wonderful, but you would be surprised how many people try to abuse it. For example, I worked for a company that would pay for round-trip tickets and seven days of leave time if it was an official approved Red Cross message. A new company took over and a new policy was put in place. The new company would allow unpaid time off for Red Cross messages and you had to buy your own ticket home. Those first few weeks it was amazing how many people cancelled their Red Cross leave and travel when they found out the company would not pay for their travel and time off.

Another time an employee had the terrible experience of unexpectedly losing his spouse. He had a young child at home and he needed to get home now! We got that Red Cross message for him and it was amazing how fast we were able to move him from his remote base.

They are not just used for commercial flights but for military flights as well. Once we showed his Red Cross Message to the military, they flew him as fast as they could by a Blackhawk chopper to our major hub and with 30 minutes to spare we had him on a flight home. This was a terrible tragedy for him but I was proud of all the people involved who dropped everything non-essential and made sure we got him home to his child.

Chapter Forty-Two

If The Unthinkable Happens

We all know that people die in a war zone but we are convinced it won't happen to us. What happens if you are killed or pass away from a health issue? If possible, most companies will send a representative to your home. Be it a spouse or your parents depends on the information you put on your emergency contact list. They may even have a professional counselor come with the company representative. Be assured an effort will be made to treat your body and personal belongings with respect.

Here's what happens: Your body will be handled by Military Mortuary Affairs. Again, if possible, a company representative will escort your body to your home of record. Your belongings will be inventoried and as neatly as possible shipped to your home of record. Nothing that is battle damaged (such as shrapnel holes or has blood on it) will be shipped home. It will be properly destroyed.

I've never forgotten my first time over here dealing with a fatality. I received a call about 6:50 in the morning. My supervisor informed me that enemy activity had killed one of our workers and would I volunteer to help search for his passport, inventory and pack his belongings. Of course, I volunteered.

I never will forget the sight I saw. Even though Mortuary Affairs had done an excellent job of clean up, there was still lots of evidence of what had happened. I and another person put on what biohazard gear we had (gloves) and started sifting through the debris one handful at a time looking for the passport. Once we had searched through a pile of whatever, we passed it to helpers outside to sort. Three piles were made. One that we felt we could ship home, another pile of battle damage, and another pile that was blood stained.

The pile we felt we could ship home was so small. The cell phone survived. While we worked, it kept ringing and ringing and ringing. We knew that it had to be loved ones and friends calling to make sure the rumor they had heard could not be true. We finally turned the cell phone off. We could not take it anymore. That cellphone was breaking our hearts.

We finished our cleanup. I took the clothing to be

shipped home over to our laundry facility. We wanted to make sure what we sent home did not have dust and dirt on them. I remember bypassing all the regular laundry workers and going straight to the supervisor. I knew I was a little emotional because of what I had just cleaned up and I kept telling the supervisor, "This man has been killed. You will treat his stuff honorably." I must have repeated myself several times and I was shaking.

He simply put his hand on my arm and said, "Derek, this is what I do. I do this every day for wounded and killed soldiers. Be assured I will treat everything with respect and it will be perfect to be shipped home." I saw in his eyes he was telling the truth. He had done this too many times. I left knowing it would be okay. I know it was just clothes, but I kept picturing the loved ones of the man pulling out each item one by one.

True to his word, the laundry supervisor called me a few hours later and said the items were ready. I picked them up and they were clean and folded professionally. I took it back to an area where we had the other small items that had survived. We cleaned the other items, such as his personal electronics. As carefully as we could, we packed everything and then took it to be shipped.

I was not there when his family got the word, when his body arrived, or when his personal belongings were unpacked. They will never know what we did to try to help ease their grief just a little. Nothing can really help all that much at a time like that, but knowing that I and all the people around me had gone the extra mile to treat his things with respect and dignity was important to me.

Chapter Forty-Three

Hope And Heartbreak

One of my favorite things to be a part of is the training of Afghan's in real marketable skills. I am proud to know I had a part in training hundreds if not thousands of Afghan's in carpentry, plumbing, heating and cooling, truck mechanics, food service, etc. My dream is one day to return to Afghanistan as a tourist. I would love to stay at a hotel "my guys" built. Eat at a restaurant that "my guys" run. Take a taxi one of "my guys" owns. Who knows what success they could see in years to come.

One of my other favorite things are the kids. I have learned from all my travels that kids are pretty much the same no matter what their country. They laugh, cry, play, and smile all the same. I got to help a bit with an orphanage/school in a small remote area. I have hope that some of those kids someday will become the leaders of their nation and will remember the Americans, Lithuanians,

Croatians, Danish, and Icelanders who tried to educate them and make their lives a little better.

At the same time your heart will be broken. Recently a 13 or 14 year old became a suicide bomber. He hit an area I am near quite often. There are always young children around. They will sell phone cards, scarfs, sunglasses, anything to make a dollar to support their families.

One little girl with the prettiest green eyes was always one of my favorites to talk to. She was nine years old, the same age as my son. Her father was crippled and she sold scarves to anyone walking by. Her English was excellent. She was so funny and could debate better than most American kids her age. Every time we would be near her corner she would always recognize us and try to sell my friend one of her very overpriced scarves! She could have sold snow to Eskimos. However, the suicide child bomber detonated his bomb at the corner where she worked selling the scarves. The best information I was able to obtain said the bomber mostly killed the children who were at that corner. I was in the area a few days later. I hoped and prayed I would see her and could buy an overpriced scarf from her. I have never seen her again.

Chapter Forty-Four

Why We Do It

Why do contractors do what they do? I have to admit I first got into it mostly for economic reasons and then my reasons turned more patriotic. I loved helping the military in my own way. They had a rule for medical care referred to as "life, limb, or sight." Anyone who was at risk of losing one of those three would have all that the military and/or company could provide to save them. I saw children brought to our front gate bleeding and burned. No movie can ever capture the heroic efforts made by the doctors, nurses, helicopter and plane pilots, and regular GI Joe and GI Jane soldiers to save those children. And it wasn't just children who were treated this way. Adults were afforded the same treatment.

I never will forget one child brought to my small base. Her parents were drug dealers. The child had accidently told someone about a truck coming that night.

Turns out it was a load of heroin. That person told someone else, and they told someone else so eventually the news made it to the police and military. They intercepted that truck. The parents were so high themselves and then so mad at the daughter that they covered her in gas and set her on fire. She was six years old. She was brought to our front gate. The doctors and nurses did everything they could.

As soon as our base found out there was a six year old burn victim fighting for her life it was buzzing with activity. Every father on that base came to me and our medic wanting to know what they could do. I was amazed at how remote our base was but yet hidden teddy bears, crayons, and coloring books suddenly appeared at my office to give to her. Our medic went to the hospital to deliver the toys. He came back in an hour with his arms still full and a heart-broken expression on his face.

He simply said, "It won't do any good." He handed me the gifts and went into his office, slowly closing the door. She died three days later. The story breaks my heart but to see what everyone did, soldier and civilian alike to try and save her, helps a little. On a side note, I don't know all the details but the parents ended up... let's just say they will never harm a child again.

Yes, there are days that break your heart but there

are countless stories of people being rescued, helped and taught.

Everyone has their own reasons for working over here. Whatever your reason, have a goal. I love hearing everyone's reason for being here. Some really pull at my heart strings.

It may be to pay for cancer treatments for a spouse or help with expenses of taking care of a special needs grandchild. You may want to visit 50 countries, pay off your house, get out of debt, etc. Always keep your eye on your goal.

Chapter Forty-Five

You Will Not Be Appreciated

A lot of people do these jobs for a patriotic reason and since you eat, sleep, and work alongside men and women in uniform in a war zone you would think you would get at least a little respect for what you do. You will not. So many times I've seen people rightfully applauding military men and women coming home at airports. People greeting them with flags and poster board signs welcoming them home.

You are not in uniform and will just walk around the celebration of these fine men and women to go on your way. Even though most soldiers are there for six months to one year, you may be doing this for years. In fact, I work with one guy who has been over here for nine years straight.

I am currently at five years in Afghanistan. Besides my immediate family, I have only once been thanked for the sacrifice I have made in supporting the troops. I never expected to be thanked or appreciated but when someone actually sent me a quick email on memorial day thanking me for what I did it actually made me stop for a minute and realize this was the first time ever I had gotten an acknowledgement and it meant a lot.

In fact, I was once having a conversation with someone I consider a best friend back home and I was mentioning that when I was finally done contracting I was going to need some time to "heal" after being in a war zone for so many years and just spend time with my family. With all seriousness, this friend said, "You're not really in a war. Why would you need time to heal?"

I would not equate what contractors do with what soldiers had to do in past wars such as the front lines of France or even with the combat soldiers of today, but you are in a war zone. At any minute car bombs could go off, rockets could come in. There are always snipers lurking about. Even watching civilians throwing rocks at your convoy takes an emotional toll. Just because you are not in uniform does not mean you are exempt from serious injury or death or won't have nerves that are completely shot by the time you leave.

Only once did I have a soldier acknowledge what we do. I was at a very remote base for two years. It was a NATO base but was supported by a US company. A high ranking US soldier came in for some business. He had been traveling to other bases that were solely run by foreign contractors or soldiers. I never will forget his comment when I greeted him. He said, "When I flew in and saw your company flag flying I knew I finally was going to get a hot shower and good food."

I lived for a year off that one comment.

I take great pride in knowing at my base a soldier always has a hot cup of coffee or cold drink, good food, and a hot shower.

Epilogue

The Future Of Overseas Contract Work

Like it or not, contracting will be here to stay for a long time. How many of those jobs exist will always depend on the conflict. It just makes economic sense for the military to use contract workers. At a moment's notice they have thousands of non-fighters ready to help with military logistics.

Who knows what country we will be in next helping to rebuild?

Acknowledgements

I'm blessed to have worked with so many talented people during my Human Resource career. They have made me laugh, cry, groan in frustration, and smile with joy when we have been given the gift of being there for our employees. I have so many to thank, but if I neglected to mention someone I am truly sorry. So in no particular order - Thank you

Professor George Oliver – Who could have thought using Lego's as a team building exercise would stick with me to this day. I am forever grateful you saw that Human Resources was the career for me.

Johnny "Rilo" Robinson – You're a good friend who told me "Sometimes you gotta just wing it" while cocking your arm in a wing shape.

Tim Fridley & Tom Zhart – You're two of the greatest bosses I've ever had and taught me people are more than numbers.

Anita Elms –Thanks for keeping me out of (HR) trouble and putting the New York smack-down on me when I needed it... or for no particular reason!

Kim Fowler – Small office or big office it just doesn't matter. Thanks for showing me servant leadership.

Theresa Petruzzelli – I didn't know you were the owner of the company until I had known you for a year. That showed me you could roll your sleeves up and get the job done.

Maria Long – During one of our many disagreements you said, "Derek, we may be dysfunctional but we are family."

Odalis Fitzpatrick, Ellen Leubbert, Samara Satterfield, Meredith Lewis, Casey Metzger, Kolene Miller, Giget Grumeretz – I know our old company mourns the day we all started going our separate ways. They had never seen a better group work together.

Elinda Boyles, Judi McGraw and Denise Gregory – Sorry you had to take down the "beefcake" calendar when I finally became the first male to join you all. So glad we survived C.A.R.S. implementation together. I miss you guys, not C.A.R.S.

Venola Riley – My Bagram sister. Another I fought with all the time but heaven help the person who came in picking a fight with either one of us from the outside. We could only talk to each other like that!

Tom Menier – Truly knows how to make someone laugh during the most stressful of times. Your secret of liking romance novels is safe with me.

Charles "Chuck" Allison – Thanks for teaching me so much about retirement plans, disability, and medical plans. Your teachings have helped me help hundreds if not thousands of people plan for a better financial future.

Chris Livingston, Sheila Hickman, Larry Welch, Frank Peloso – Showed me that those at the Ivory Tower do have hearts.

John Jordan, Brent Farmer, and Chris Hodge – I know you slept better at night knowing "Thunder and Lightning" was there to protect you.

Miguel Mireles and Paul Tadlock – Minus 60 windchill, counting afghani money every payroll together, drug lords launching rockets at us, time sheet inspections every week and sneaking food to the orphans. How could you not become "brothers" through all that.

Dwayne Taylor – "Derek, no matter what – that plane will not take off until our guy is on board." Needless to say that plane did not take off until he was on there. Thanks for teaching me to be cool in stressful times.

Dave Tate – One of the most amazing recruiters I ever worked with.

Marsha Mills – Giving me my first big break. I will always be grateful.

Catherine Stanley – Amazing to learn together that be it England, USA, or Afghanistan we all have the same HR challenges.

Shabir Ahmad – Turned down other jobs just to work with me. Willing to go to jail when it looked like I was going. How you humbled me and taught me the culture of Afghanistan.